INDEX

First published by
Everything Written cc in 2011

100 Raubernheir Street, Heilbron
Free State, South Africa, 9650

Tel: +27 (0)83 375 8176
http://www.everythingwritten.co.za

ISBN 978-0-620-51922-9

The National Library of South Africa Data
Kitshoff, Heidi,
Déjà vu You / Heidi Kitshoff.

The National Library of South Africa in Publication Data
A catalogue record for this book is available from The National Library of South Africa.

Printed in South Africa by Mega Digital (Pty) Ltd.

DÉJÀ VU YOU

Heidi Kitshoff

<u>ACKNOWLEDGEMENT</u>

I want to thank all my friends, family and a few old boyfriends for the help, inspiration, tears and laughter you provided to awaken my senses and capture the moments and feelings on paper.

A special thanks to Sean, for making me believe in myself and to keep reaching for my dream. Thanks for never giving up on me.

And to Lauren. You're suffering from a great illness, but still took some of your precious "spoons" to create this beautiful cover. Thank you.

And all Praise to God for the gift He gave me.

Mom and Dad.......

This book is dedicated to you.

SENSES

Looking into your eyes – is like seeing it for the first time,

A new sunrise.

Seeing you smile – makes me wish time would freeze,

Only for a little while.

Feeling your touch – makes my skin tingle,

Can never feel too much.

Hearing your voice – is my song for the day

By choice.

You are an experience that's impossible to forget.

You make love an amazing game to play.

You are the fun part of my day.

Oh what I would do, to make you stay.

THE ARTIST

Captivated by your words

Drowning in your eyes

Excited by your smile

Moved by your touch

Simple words capturing

The simplicity of the beauty within

Your deep words will echo

Through my mind for time to come

Reminding me of a beauty

Locked up in sound

Your blue eyes looked deep

Entering where not allowed to pass

Seeing me from the inside

No judgement on what was found

Your smile so cute

Emphasising a mouth to be kissed

Rounded off by lips

That moves thee within

Your fingers move in ways

And ways that moves me

Skin on skin

A touch remained imprinted

Experiencing the art of an artist

He's canvas; me

A wonderful work of art was laid

Upon the soul of me

...He's brush is he's presence

MOVING PAST EACH OTHER

For years, you have been the centre of my dreams

You were the idol I looked up to

You were the one in who's arms I longed to be wrapped in

Your attention and love is what I craved

For a long time

I was happy with the scraps that I was given

As long as they came from you

You still thought of me

Then things changed

Your life changed

And it seemed I started playing a more important part

I started to matter

And then one day

Rather unexpected

I went from an option

To be your priority

My dreams came true

My waiting paid off

I got you

You're mine

But....it seems that over time

I too have changed

And I don't think I'm what you want

And I don't think you are what I need

<u>STILL NOT OVER YOU</u>

It's hard to accept it

It's hard to move on

All that I'm hearing

Is the words of a sad song

Feeling left alone

Out in the cold

No one to care for

No one to hold

It's been days

I should be over this

But still I desire

The deepness of your kiss

Tell me what's your secret

How did you forget

I long for freedom

If only my heart would let

I wish I could be like you

And just easily move on

So that I can now whistle too

The tune of a happy song

<u>...NOT EVEN A GOOD BYE</u>

Anger, Hurt, Pain

Who is to blame?

I opened the door

Wanted more

Three in the morn

Lying in bed torn

You nowhere to found

My thoughts being hound

Can't be cross with you

I should have knew

The joke is on me

I'm the fool to be!

SICK

I heard a bug

Crawled in your mug

While sipping your morning tea.

Now you're blue

With tummy flu

And a fever to some degree.

Hoping you recover soon

Moving on from your sick gloom

So strong you'll feel again.

So take care of yourself

Look at your health

Till again we see you when.

LET IT GO

Nails pinch hard

Your grip is tight

You're not letting go

Your holding on with might

You've put your life on the line

You've put your life on hold

You've put your heart out there

It wasn't good enough, you've been told.

You're holding on to hopes

You're holding on to dreams

You're holding on to memories

It's all a haze it seems.

As the mist of confusion clears up

You're left with reality

And the hopes and dreams fade away.

Were they really something to hold on to?

We're they ever there?

We're they ever true?

And your realise; what are you holding on to?

Let it go. Let it go!

It's time to let it go.

Let go of the memories

Let go of the hopes

Let go of the good

Let it go!

Let go of the cuddling

Let go of the hugs

Let go of the kisses

Let of the smile

Let go of the wishes

Let it go!

It only hurts for a while

So

Let go of the past

Let go of the years

Let go of the hurt

Let go of the tears.

Wipe your eyes and stand up,

Face the world and let it go!

MISUNDERSTOOD

Why am I so misunderstood?

Misread?

Misquoted?

My intention all good

Why not perceived as that?

Am I doing it wrong?

How must I do it right?

I'm lost,

Confused,

Misunderstood.

SMILE

Words fail me.

How do you write a smile?

Punctuation overrated.

How do you print a smile?

Laughter dancing in my heart,

But only visible in my smile.

Butterflies circle my tummy,

But across my face a smile.

A million happy thought cross my mind,

But the only proof my smile.

Thousands of thankful prayers leaving my soul

And the evidence is in my smile.

Locked up in a single smile

So much that is good.

You too can portray what is positive,

Simply just smile.

WALKING AWAY

Empty heart... Empty you

No feelings inside, only colours of blue

Empty soul... Empty life

Words that hurt, cut like a knife

Hope you're happy now

For no longer at your feet I bow

Hope you're satisfied

Looked me in the eye and lied

Hope your new life is filled with love

I'll just wait for grace from above

Hope your new life is filled with joy

Thinking how you used me like a toy

Hope this is what you really want

Hope this is what you really need

Now there is no looking back or turning away

It was your choice, so with her you'll have to stay

For my heart of diamonds and love as precious as gold

To someone else faithful it will be sold

Because you don't deserve it

Not a single piece of my soul

Because you're the one who dumped me in this black hole.

LOOSING MYSELF

I lost something dear to me

It had zest for life

Sparkle and sunshine

And confidence to climb a mountain

It had the strength to stand in storms

And the compassion for those in need

It had endless love to give

And an unstoppable passion for fun

It was daring and adventurous

And always up for a dare

Going to sleep was no option

Cos it had too much life to live

A party wasn't a party without it there

And a party never ended till the next morning

It enjoyed nature to the full

And overflowed with thanks to God

I miss it terribly

Life just isn't the same

Where to start looking for it

Where did it go

I lost something dear to me

I lost myself.

THE MOTH

A tiny Moth is sitting on the wall. Its wings so delicate that even a soft breeze could tear them.

Silently the Moth sits on the wall, glancing at the warm light coming from beneath.

A candle's Flame is lighting up the whole room, touching every dark corner.

It's a warm flow that fills the room and the light it gives plays softly on the wings of the Moth.

The feel of this is so tempting and inviting it causes the Moth to lose every ounce of sanity.

The Moth lets go of the steady wall, the wall that was safe and far away from the intoxicating Flames.

The Moth wonders nearer to the Flame, inspecting it and the closer it goes the warmer it gets.

It's the most amazing feeling the Moth has ever experienced.

As the Moth flies around the candle, the Moth and Flame dance with each other, creating the most beautiful shadows on the wall.

All the time, the Moth is moving closer and closer, the warmth of the Flame is so addictive and provoking, it can't be avoided.

And then...the Moth goes to close. The Moth's wings flame up and burn until none is left and the Moth drops to the ground.

The Moth looks up at the warm Flame with tears and questions and confusion...

It's not understood how something so warm, so beautiful, can hurt so much?

And why would it after the beautiful memories that were left in the shadows on the wall?

With no wings and a broken spirit the Moth looks up at the Flame, still wanting to be close to it, yet it can never be.

Life for the Moth has changed forever but still the memory of the warm, glowing Flame, remains in the heart of the Moth...still wanting...still needing...not knowing how to carry on without it.

You are the Flame, and I am the Moth.

TO MY LOVE ON VALENTINE'S DAY

It's Valentine's Day and all is filled with love.

Friends and family and blessings from above.

Blessed we are to have one another,

To be love and be together.

But between you and me, our hearts are empty,

Love has faded and moments are lonely.

Things between us aren't as they used to be,

And scary thoughts cross our minds to be set free.

Thinking back at all we've had

And seeing how quickly the world has gone bad,

Made me realise to rather hold on tight,

Keep what I have and give flight.

I'm sure when I say; give love a chance,

That you feel the same and will snap from your trance.

Let's take this day and find what we've lost,

Do whatever we have to, no matter the cost.

Let's fall in love again, give it another try,

Lie in each other's arms and dream into the starry sky.

This Valentine's Day I give you my heart again.

I will try to make things better and let you forget the pain.

All I ask is for you to love me back,

Together this will work and get us back on track.

WAITING

Time ticking away at its own pace.

Waiting is a game for professionals.

Minutes' drive you crazy,

Hours flames insanity...

And still you wait for that one thing.

One special thing

That would make time irrelevant.

That one dearest thing

That consumes your mind and senses.

Oh how you long for that one important thing;

Important, because you made it your personal idol.

While waiting,

So much can be done, enjoyed and accomplished.

But everything seems like nothing

When you're waiting for that one thing.

WHAT IF...

What if I told you I don't want to wait anymore...

What if I told you I don't want to be alone...

What if I told you my arms feel empty with no one to hold...

What if I told you my lips feel dry with no one to kiss...

What if I told you my bed is empty with no one to keep me warm from the cold...

What if I told you my soul is dead with no one to share a special wish...

What if I told you my heart is lonely, longing for someone to love...

What if I told you life is too short to have these empty feelings.

What if I told you that when I met you all this emptiness were gone.

What if I tell you I think you're the one!

If God gives you a moment, take it and don't let it slip away.

Life is too short.

Life is too short for "what ifs".

To out and live life and love life.

If you feel love, share love.

<u>GONE</u>

It's been over for months

But my home and life were still filled with you.

Where I went of who I met,

There was always a piece of you in everything.

I tried blocking you out,

Moving on,

Moving you out

But you always in some way or another, remained.

But today you were here in flesh.

Today you came yourself,

And moved you out of my life.

I wasn't prepared for how hard it would actually be.

I had no idea it would still hurt.

I had no idea how much it would hurt.

And now you're gone.

I look around me and you're gone.

My house is empty,

My home is empty,

My life is empty.

You're actually gone

And I wasn't prepared for that.

I had no idea it would feel this empty.

You are really gone.

<u>ON OUR WEDDING DAY</u>

God is love, and love brought us together. From the rib of Adam a partner were brought to life.

With the love of God, we are made to fit together like a puzzle, to form the most beautiful picture of all; our future together, and that beautiful journey starts today.

TO MY WIFE

Every morning I wake up

You're the first one that I see

This is how I want it

This is how it should be

I thank you for being

The better half to me

I thank you for your love

You give to me so free

I love you my darling

I love you my wife

I can't imagine living

Without you in my life

WHAT MATTERS

Prioritise

Minimise

Take only what you need

Faith

Hope

Food for the soul to feed

Love

Respect

Morals dear

Family

Friends

Keep loved ones near

Beauty

Purity

Look for the good out there

Patience

Kindness

Always play fair

EASY WAY OUT

Used and second hand

You had your fun

Easiest way out

Is to turn and run

Oh what a pity

A memory like this

Had to end this way

Not even a kiss

Disappointed, rejection

Hard facts to face

Within the sweetness of you

Didn't think I'd find a trace

But here I stand again

Alone

How easy you turned your back

And away you have flown.

GETTING DOWN GETTING UP

I will not let this get me down

Today is too sunny and bright

To be wearing a frown

Ok, so things didn't go my way

But strong I must be,

From my goal I must not stray

The news I got wasn't what I wanted to hear

Strong I'll stay,

My situation I will not fear

I can't just give up

Believe I have to

Overflow one day will be my cup

But it's not that easy to stand strong

When you feel

All that goes is wrong

Faith is what I need to get me through the day

Who knows...

Tomorrow things might just go my way

So I'll try to turn away from sad

Close my eyes

And not look at the bad

Keep the faith that tomorrow is mine

Hoping and praying

Tomorrow for me the sun will shine

NOTHING

Second hand

Thrown away

Used

Nothing

Worthless

Emotionally abused

Empty

Dead

Hurt

Sad

Broken

Lower than dirt

BROWN

- Inspired by my curtains...

Brown, a colour dull and dead to the eye.

A colour taken for granted

As being so plain,

It just automatically blends in unnoticed

But have you ever taken a closer look?

Have you ever taken the time to look beyond the obvious?

Brown, a mixture of rainbow colours,

Lively colours bonding to form this shade.

So, yet not colourful

It holds all the elements of all the colours mixed

Making it richer than gold,

Sunnier than yellow

And lovelier than red.

Brown, the colour of hope and growth

As from the brown soil of your fertile earth

Springs life in its most beautiful form.

WRITING TODAY

Finally have the time

But can't find the words to rhyme

Have to get this book done

Respect to be won

Oh what to write next?

Maybe modern technology ,text?

That not making sense

Getting more tense

Something blocking my mind

Inspiration hard to find

My goal is set

But will it be met?

Open up, words to flow

Must give this a go

Today this is no use

Just giving my mind abuse

Will try again tomorrow

Hope there's inspiration to follow

<u>HEY JAY</u>

You say you don't have space for me in your life,

Yet you fill up all of mine.

You constantly run through the grassy fields of my mind.

You nestle softly in the feathers of my heart.

You walk beside the rivers of my thoughts.

You dance on the beat of my heart.

The short time spent together,

Moved all mountains within me

And by taking your love away,

It's like every breath is a hammer beating those mountains down...

Crumbling away at my deepest emotions.

So although I still feel for you very deeply

And I do wish you well,

I do wish you would disappear...

Disappear from my thoughts...

From my dreams...

From my heart.

SPECIAL MOMENTS TREASURED

You left as quick as you came

But the footprints you left behind

Won't for long be forgotten.

Like a warm summers' breeze,

You swept across my face.

Leaving featherlike tinglings

Around the corners of my mouth

As I smile at the thought of you

Being in my arms.

Brief was the moment we shared

But lasting the touch you left on my heart.

Sadden I am

Your you leaving like you came.

But comforted by the essence you left behind.

Never again I might walk

In the clouds as I do today.

But pray for a brief moment

That by being me,

I touched a small piece of your soul too.

YOUR PROBLEM

It's not my problem,

So don't make it mine.

And if it was my problem,

I'll make it yours.

Don't dump your junk on me.

Keep your garbage to yourself.

No one really listens

And the world does not care.

Dry your tears,

And toughen up.

Straighten your back

And face your hand of cards dealt.

Get over yourself.

You're no more special than me.

So pack up your tears,

And walk your own destiny.

STRONG AND MOVING ON

I'll be strong

I'll move on

It won't be long

Till again I'm strong.

All hasn't ended

Me you offended

Left my heart bended

I repeat, all hasn't ended.

Today I might cry

Tomorrow give it another try

Look up to the sky

Find new wings to fly.

Knew it wouldn't last

Putting you in the past

Moving on fast

Moving on fast

So good bye to you

No longer I'm blue

Finding someone true

And it's not you.

OUR FRIENDSHIP

A new friend I found

Bundled up in you

My lonely days of hardship

Is finally through

Dependable you are

Funny and caring

Maybe at times sad

But always daring

And now I've gone and messed it up

Treated you like dirt

Once your were my best friend

Now I've put you third

I'm sorry for the way I was

I'm sorry for what I've done

I'm sorry I pushed you aside

I know it was wrong

Please accept my apology

Accept my word of sorry

Please save our friendship

And tell me not to worry

Please don't take it away

Our dearest friendship sweet

Please don't make and end to it

For surely I will weep

<u>TAKING MINE BACK</u>

I see the lives of so many people wash out on the beach.

Roll on, shoes and a little boy's dream.

Rolling in the waves, are everyday life...

A house that was built, a home that is now empty.

God created earth, God created man.

It all was given to us to develop in His honour.

To build and protect and share with each other in love.

So man built and developed and built even more,

But greed and hate took the place

Where love was meant to be shared.

All that was built was in beauty

But the hearts that filled these homes were empty.

Empty of love.

Empty of God.

As all creation can only stand so much,

God Himself has had enough!

For all He had given was used and abused.

Not part of the goal that was once set.

So God came to claim His land back.

He took it in a forceful sweep.

As the waves came crashing in,

Breaking down all that is built.

Sin too was demolished and washed out to sea.

Devastation is left.

Homes are gone and lives that were built are washed away.

As I sit and watch the crashing of the waves,

I wonder if man will make the same mistakes again?

Or has the hourglass been turned for God to come once more...

And claim His land back?

TEARS FALL LIKE WORDS

The hurt you cause me,

I use as inspiration.

How sick is that?

How pathetic have you made me?

As you bring tears to my life,

The words roll out too.

As you make my heart ache

My hand goes to paper.

The smiles you brought to my life,

Was never enough to share.

Yet the hurt you brought

Feeds enough tears to rain on all mankind.

So a silly question it is indeed;

Is the heart ache really needed

If the smiles were so few

And the love one sided?

But as my words,

My tears roll out the answer

In clear pathways of truth;

You can't tell your heart who not to love.

JUDGING DIFFERENCES

What is right

What is wrong

Who are you to judge

I don't like fat

But what if that's my fate?

Am I going to hate myself?

You don't like blondes

Who cares if they have more fun

Brunettes just don't tell

So what if I like blue

Green doesn't suit you

It's all part of the same rainbow anyway

We're all different

We're all unique

But don't be so quick to judge

As we're all part of the same life

"I'm not old, I'm a recycled teenager"

~ Quote on a T-Shirt

ONE LAST ONE

As I flip through these pages I note,

Many lovers have indeed crossed my path.

Many a time before my heartfelt the warm beating of being in love.

My photo albums overflow

With different faces that has come and gone over the years.

Each individual leaving me with memories.

Memories of happy days.

Memories of sad moments too.

Oh how many have I loved over the years.

Maybe we all are meant to only have

A certain amount of lovers in our lifetime.

And maybe I have reached my limit.

But oh, only one more please,

Just one last butterfly feeling in the depts of my stomach.

Just one more hand to fold around mine

And stay there till the end of time.

LUPUS

For Lauren

Your pain I can't feel

But your suffering I can see

Watching you wither away to that deadly disease

Me helpless on the side-line

It's a sin

It's cruel that you were chosen

To be the one

Wearing this deadly crown

A free spirit

Loving all that lives

Seeing passion in life

But trapped in death you're bound

You deserve so much more

For you know the precious of life

You need to heal

For you need to live full

I'm holding your hand

I'm touching your heart

I'm praying for you

I'm loving you

More I wish I could do for you

But how little do I really understand

How little do I know of your suffer

How could I ever comprehend

I'm uneducated

And experience in this pain I lack

But I'll keep standing next to you

and love you with all I have.

SECOND CHANCE

Maybe you haven't noticed,

But dearly I love you true.

But something is amiss,

As all I do is make you blue

Maybe if I try harder,

What if I try again?

But will you let me do this,

On your answer it depends.

Should I love you different?

Should I care another way?

Will any of this matter,

Will any of this make you stay?

Force you I can't do.

Blame you is not fair.

I leave this in your hands now,

And remember to take care.

LOSING A LOVED ONE

The news just came.

I'm so sorry my friend.

Seeing you hurt like that,

Wish your heart I could mend.

This morning when you woke,

You didn't think it would happen today.

Although you know it's meant to be,

You still wished it wouldn't come your way.

I pray for comfort.

May The Lord keep you near,

Wipe all your tears

And all those to you near.

I'm sorry for your loss,

I can offer my shoulder to cry.

Be strong my friend,

It will get better as time goes by...

But unfortunately all of us one day has to die.

SMURFIE

I love you my baby

I love you really true

Although at times

We seem to make each other blue

Things don't always go as planned

Sometimes we just make each other sad

But through it all

Things aren't always bad

Many times over, we experience the good

Love, laughter, fun to mention but a few

None of which would be possible

If the other person weren't you

Support you give me plenty

And a strong hand to keep me up

A chocolate in my lunch tin

A smile in my morning coffee cup

Don't ever doubt the good you do

Or the positive part you play

I'm happy to have you near me

And hope you are here to stay

HOLIDAY ROMANCE

For a moment in time

The luckiest girl I was

As you walked into my life

And returned the sparkle to my eyes

You moved me

You touched me

Kissed my lips

And enflamed all my senses

You made my heart beat faster

You made my heart stop

With every glance of you

You made my heart skip a beat

For years I've longed

For passion that burns so deep

And today I'm the lucky one

Who will receive

You moved me to places

Made me escape this world

In a dream I was dancing

Every time I looked into your eyes

As pen goes to paper

My dripping eyes remind me

That this romance so rare

Is not to be kept forever

We were given precious seconds

And made them last for days

But now the sadness comes

As we part our own ways

My heart is sore

Having to let you go

My insides are breaking

I just want you to know

But when at night

In bed I close my eyes

My dreams will be of you

Recalling each sweet memory

In my thoughts

And in my heart

Forever you will be

Thank you dear baby

For picking me.

<u>FAMILY</u>

We... I... sometimes take them for granted because they're just always there and around. Never have I thought of the day this union would be broken. When there would be an empty chair at the dinner table... I'm so blessed, where others shed tears, for I get to have all my loved ones near.

Alone I don't have to eat my dinner, as we place our hands in one another to say thanks to the Gracious Lord above. I don't have to cry alone, although my pain I would want to hide from the ones who see into my soul. Yet, they are the ones with the unlimited comfort an no words of judgment.

Support, actually just another form of love, is as strong as the brick walls keeping us safe at night. Caring and sharing together, celebrating our blessings of having each other near. Sadly, dark days and pain creep in too. We are all only human after all. But the bond and blood flowing deep in our hearts and veins, always brings us back together again. Back together in our safe unity, our family.

A ROSE, THE ROSE

Isn't a Rose beautiful?

From a distance, almost perfect.

But look closer....it is not!

We all have our bruises and flaws,

Even something as beautiful as a Summer's Rose in full bloom.

Here and there you might find some of the leaves' colour,

Fades away or even a leaf that didn't quite develop

To contribute to being perfect.

And then there is the thorns.

They're ugly and it doesn't make sense

Why such a beautiful thing should have something so ugly,

Sharp and hurtful?

So what do you do with your Rose?

You are the master of it.

You picked it so there for you can sculpt it to your hand

And your own perfection.

You pick off the ugly leaves, pulling them out one by one.

A dew drop runs down the palm of your hand,

You don't notice it's a tear from the agony and pain the Rose is experiencing.

The poor Rose is crying out for you to stop,

For the pain is unbearable!

Still you proceed, snipping off the thorns one by one

Until you are happy with your creation.

You've formed the perfect Rose, one that suites you in all your needs,

And you smile.

You are the master of this creation,

You modelled it to your own perfection.

You put it in some water and up on the table

Where you can look at it and enjoy the sight of it.

But something doesn't seem right...

You take a closer look...

This isn't a Rose anymore!

Half of its' leaves are missing and it doesn't have any thorns!

The sweet smell is gone and it's head started to hang

From all the pain it had to undergo during the reforming process.

Yes, you thought you were the master of this Rose,

But in actual fact, you were the one blessed to find this creation God had left you

And now you made it into something it's not.

How sad it is, for you will never find this Rose again,

This colour with this smell.

And you realise that the faded leaves were all part of the "perfect" picture

And the thorns were for it's own protection.

Something so good and pure and beautiful

Has to have protection from the cruel outside world.

So you are left with a choice;

Sit with your deformed creation

Or toss it aside.

Pick another rose

And try not to make the same mistake again.

Appreciate it for what it is,

For what God had given you.

BEING DIFFERENT ISN'T WRONG

How can this be right

If all I do is getting it wrong,

Through your eyes the picture you see.

From the day in the start

You knew different I was to you

But pursued you still did.

Was it for the fantasy?

A challenge maybe to you,

Or did true potential creep up on you?

Now time down the line

The differences too far moves,

Like continents of countries far.

My character constantly being attacked.

My motives questioned.

My words insulted.

Breaking down my will.

Slashing my self-esteem.

Pushing to a lower form of being.

Maybe you don't mean the harm.

Criticism to build my strength.

Wisdom for the path ahead.

Accept the fact that different I'll be,

And that being different

Doesn't make me wrong.

Accept my bad with my good,

Take me a package in whole.

There is always a shadow with light.

By constantly shutting me out of being me,

You're killing my spark to life,

Taking away all I stand and live for.

For being me isn't fun anymore.

Constantly being challenged in my own character,

Reminder of my flaws.

So once again I ask you sweet,

My differences to be unique.

Respect them for what they are

And remember;

Being different, doesn't make me wrong.

<u>GIVING UP</u>

When to give up hope?

When time is against you...

When you've failed too many times?

How long must you hold on?

When is enough, enough?

Isn't hope just dreams?

And shouldn't they stay just that?

Where do you draw the line?

When do you accept?

How do you accept....

So kill hope!

And dream when you're asleep!

I'M HAPPY FOR YOU

For years you got the least

The least attention

The least boyfriends

The least best of you

Amen to changing times

As the wheel do turn

Dark does become light

The cloud does have a silver lining

I'm happy for you

You deserve this

I'm happy for you

You deserve only the best

Damn the changes

And I wish the wheel would break off

Blow out that candle for Eskom

Let the sun drive the clouds away

Now I'm the one longing

For my happy days to come

I'm the one waiting

For my ship to come in

But I'm happy for you

You deserve this

I'm happy for you

You deserve the best

Now I'm the least popular

My dreams back in the queue

My happy is on hold

Till further a due

But I'm truly happy for you

You deserve this

I'm happy for you

You deserve the best.

"Perseverance: The courage to ignore the obvious wisdom of turning back"

~ On a Motivation Poster

MOTHERHOOD

The beauty of motherhood is special and truly rare.

A gift or task, few of us would consider or dare.

You were chosen and blessed to bring into this world

A new life, the value too much to ever be sold.

For years you have waited, prayed for the day,

When God heard you and blessed you, bringing motherhood your way.

Excitement grows in your eyes and heart as the baby inside you form.

Counting the days and hours till your little baby is born.

A good mother you will be as all you have to give is love.

God made you that way, this was sent from above.

Take care of your family and the life you give new,

For gifts as special as this are rare and only given to Gods' few.

FRIENDSHIP

Made up from two words: friend and ship.

And I believe that it's just that.

Me and each of you, my friends, are together on a ship or a boat or a yacht or a cruise liner, on an adventure into the future.

We travel together and on our journey together we make the most beautiful of memories.

Some of you are on a yacht with me.

My adventure seeking friends. Let the wind take its course and blow us where the fun is.

I appreciate your enthusiasm and lust for life and how you put all your trust in God, that His wind will blow us where we are meant to be.

Others are on a row boat with me.

Times are tough but we seem to stick by each other on this journey, for this too has a destination.

This boat is for the friends that were so close to me when my dad was so ill.

We were thrown into a little row boat, but you helped me to row to shore.

And then there's some friends who's relaxing in the sun on a cruise liner.

It's nice to have you too, to enjoy the finer things in life and marvel at its pleasures.

Thanks for all the fun times together.

Thank you for your friend"ship".

May the waves of change, and the tides of glory move us to greatness in our journey together.

And may God forever be our Lighthouse, lighting the way for us as we set sail on the seas of life.

Photo 8: Heidi Kitshoff

FALLING IN LOVE

Looking up into the dark evening sky

Thousands of little twinkling stars spell out your name

Each one bright and beautiful, a universe on its own

If you close your eyes, you can swear they're calling out to you

Their heavenly beauty flows down from the sky

And covers your body, mind and soul

And surrounds your heart in a tight grip

A grip so tight even the air in your lungs escape

How long you've longed for this beauty to become yours

How long have you waited for the moment to be yours

Endless lonely nights, dreaming about what others have

And what you're not blessed to experience

The moment is overwhelming

Your breath is lost

Your heart skips a beat

Your tummy fill with the flutter of tiny wings

Yes yes yes

This is it

This is what you've been waiting for

Yes yes yes

With much effort you open your eyes from the dream

And decide to grip this experience tight

This one , you're not going to let go

This one, was made for you

You stand up with pride

Head held high

And you reach

You stretch out your arm and reach into the starry sky

Further and further you stretch your arm

But.....

The glorious stars spelling out your name

Is out of reach

It's too far

And no effort from within will allow you to touch them

To pick them one by one

And to make them your own.

FOR KATJA

Years ago, a friend walked into my life

Planting footsteps deep

And careful impressions

As from cut by a knife

Your presence in my life till now

Words fail to support

Expression even limited

To the single word "wow"

Through times of hard

And moments of dark

Support you gave

Your hand to find, not hard

Sunshine times there were lots too

Happy days to share

Beautiful memories made

'cos by my side were you

Although now we might be worlds apart

Contact few and words are short

But both us know

You're in my heart

So I hope with time passing

Closer we will get

'cos friend you're and angel

A friendship everlasting

DREAMING PAST THE OBVIOUS

One day, met someone not knowing,

Not imagining or thinking past the obvious.

A glance that took a second, lasted for years,

Not knowing it then.

As the hands of time ticked on,

The image in my mind was visited on occasion.

Now wondering, but still not knowing.

Not looking past the obvious, but deeply craving it.

Situations made me put the image and all feelings attached

In a box called; Dreams.

Still thinking of the obvious,

Knowing its boundaries.

But as situations rule our lives

We are forced at times to open boxes that are sealed,

Even the ones marked; Dreams,

Just so that we can hold on.

I looked inside that box and took out that image,

Craving the feelings attached

And also the unknown to it.

Now I'm dreaming past the obvious

And hope that it doesn't have the boundaries I've set for it.

Still not knowing the outcome,

But knowing it's possible,

I ask of you, image printed in my head,

Move from my box of dreams into my heart.

Erase the obvious,

Break the boundaries

And make me come alive.

DARK DAYS OF MARCH

Darkened my soul by the dwelling of hurt

Blackened my heart by desertion

Alone in my cave

I choose to hide from the sun

Cold stone walls my chosen company

Hard wet floor as cold as my thoughts

No fire needed or required

By choice vent the evil in the cold

Do not seek for now

Hope in my empty eyes

Do not offer now

Comfort for my tortured heart

All has a place in the circle of life

Each piece will fit in it's own time

Now shall be the era of the cold

For that too has a place to live

<u>DEAR LORD</u>

Dear Lord, I pray to You today

I pray to thank You for making things go my way,

For bringing her back and making her stay.

I thank You for giving me another chance, another try,

For You have seen my tears and heard me cry,

But now all that sorrow has gone by.

Thank You for bringing us back together,

I hope this time is forever

And aprt again never.

Help me to lover her right,

To avoid every fight

And teach me to hold her tight.

Help me to see

With open eyes and open heart how she loves me,

With everything that lets her be.

Teach me to appreciate even though I don't always understand,

That by the way she touches my hand,

It's her way of strengthening our band.

Help me to feel what she's trying to show,

Although there might be times I'm not sure and I don't know,

That this is her way of making our love grow.

Show me how to love her true,

Even in times when we both feel blue,

To remind her I'm stuck to her like glue.

Dear Lord, once again I pray to say thanks that we are together,

Your Name I carry in my heart forever

And that in love, we fail You never.

Amen.

CHARLIE

Told you I'd write to you

A poem one day.

Printed on paper,

Words I can't find to say.

A special place inside my heart

You've found to hide.

A secret place I can run too,

To shut out what's outside.

You've been my ultimate fantasy,

You've been my every dream.

You've been all that I've needed

When life was worse than it seem.

You've been what I've longed for,

Every thought you've crossed.

You've been my great escape

When everything I've lost.

To me if there was perfect,

Molded into you it would be.

Thanks for being amazing,

Thanks for setting my soul free.

You are truly wonderful,

Special you'll always be.

Thanks for being you

And for touching deep inside of me.

A GIRLS' DREAM

Every girl has a dream

Why can't I have too?

A white dress, flowers

And something blue.

Sweeping down the aisle

Your husband to be wait,

Eternal promises to make,

Is this my fate?

Building a home

Building a life

Together forever.

Will I be a wife?

White picket fence,

Raising a family.

How long to wait

For my desire happily?

www.ingramcontent.com/pod-product-compliance
Lightning Source LLC
Chambersburg PA
CBHW050959050726
47592CB00007B/2641